Please return on or before the latest date above.
You can renew online at www.kent.gov.uk/libs
or by phone 08458 247 200

CUSTOMER SERVICE EXCELLENCE

Libraries & Archives

Kent
County
Council

feed their imagination

funky lunch
happy food for happy children

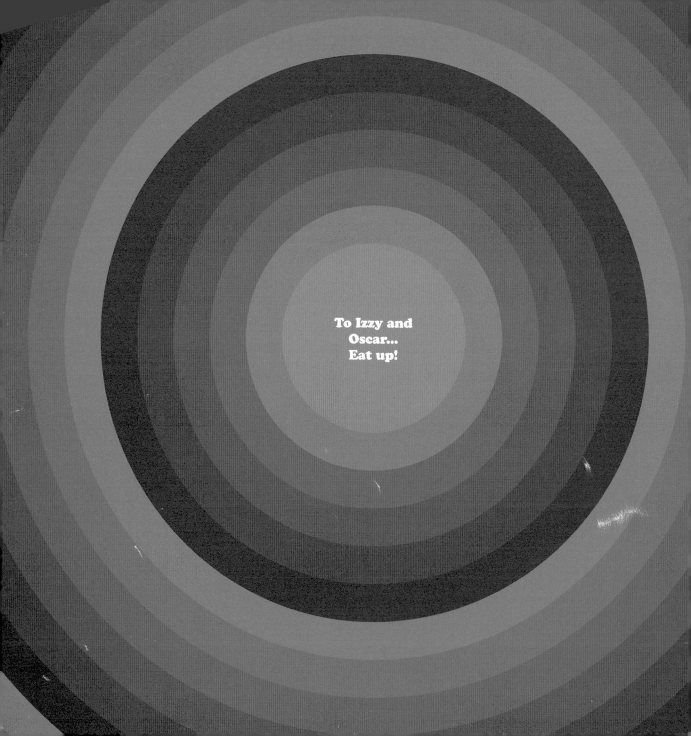

To Izzy and
Oscar...
Eat up!

funky lunch

happy food for happy children

mark northeast

absolute press A.

First published in Great Britain in 2010 by
Absolute Press
Scarborough House
29 James Street West
Bath BA1 2BT
Phone 44 (0) 1225 316013
Fax 44 (0) 1225 445836
E-mail info@absolutepress.co.uk
Website www.absolutepress.co.uk

Publisher Jon Croft
Commissioning Editor Meg Avent
Design Matt Inwood & Claire Siggery
Photography Matt Inwood
Editorial Assistant Andrea O'Connor

ISBN 9781906650308
Printed and bound in Italy by Jeming SRL

A catalogue record of this book is available from
the British Library.

A note about the text This book was set using
Cooper Black and Helvetica Neue. Cooper Black
was designed by Oswald Bruce Cooper and first
produced by Barnhart in 1922, and acquired in
1924 by the Schriftguß AG in Dresden. Helvetica
was designed in 1957 by Max Miedinger of the
Swiss-based Haas foundry. In the early 1980s,
Linotype redrew the entire Helvetica family.
The result was Helvetica Neue.

funky lunch

visit the
website:
www.funkylunch.com
or e-mail:
munch@funkylunch.com
or follow on Twitter:
@funkylunch
or join on Facebook

which sandwich?

11 rocket 13 caterpillar 15 pirate ship
17 ice cream 19 flowers 21 crocodile
23 spider 25 house 27 pig 29 sheep
31 mermaid 33 train 35 owl
37 butterfly 39 nessy 41 giraffe
43 lion 45 birthday cake 47 monkey
49 fish 51 reindeer 53 shark 55 parrot
57 cat 59 rabbit 61 octopus 63 cow
65 clown 67 crab 69 alien 71 chicken
73 piano 75 kite 77 snail 79 submarine

in the beginning...

'Don't play with your food!' was the usual response from my parents as I sat at the table as a child mindlessly pushing food around my plate in a daydream. I was a bit of a fussy eater and would turn my nose up at most things my mother put in front of me at meal times, especially if it contained 'greens'.

Fast forward some 30 years, and as a parent I wondered if I too would experience such epic battles of defiance between a child and a plate of food. Luckily I was blessed with children who would try something at least once, but from experience I know that meal times are never straight forward in any household.

The idea for Funky Lunch started as a bit of fun, a way to cheer up a grumpy four-year-old who didn't want anything for lunch one day. I could have just let him go without, but decided to try and put a smile on his face and cut his sandwich into a space rocket shape. The result was an instant hit with a big smile and an empty plate.

Always up for a challenge, I decided to continue these mini sandwich feasts on a regular basis and it soon became a talking point online with friends on Facebook asking what was coming next. I tried to make each new sandwich better than the last and something that would appeal to my children,

but I had rules, every one was made using ingredients found in the fridge and should contain as much fruit and veg as I could get in to the design, and one last rule, the most important, it had to be eaten... all of it.

I set up a website for Funky Lunch displaying my 'works of art', as they were being called, and the media soon picked up on it. In a very short space of time, it became a global news story with people talking about Funky Lunch from as far afield as Brazil, China, Canada and Australia. Appearances on television made me realise just how much interest it was generating and parents worldwide were emailing to say thank you for helping with their food dilemmas.

It's almost been a year since I made that first sandwich, to today that I'm writing this introduction for my book... my Funky Lunch book! In that time I have spoken to many people, families who have spread the word and parents who believe in what Funky Lunch set out to achieve... happy food for happy children.

So whether you are catering for a little one's birthday party, trying to broaden their taste buds, struggling with a picky eater or you just want to put a smile on a grumpy four year old, I hope Funky Lunch will give you the inspiration to try something different, encourage better eating and feed their imagination.

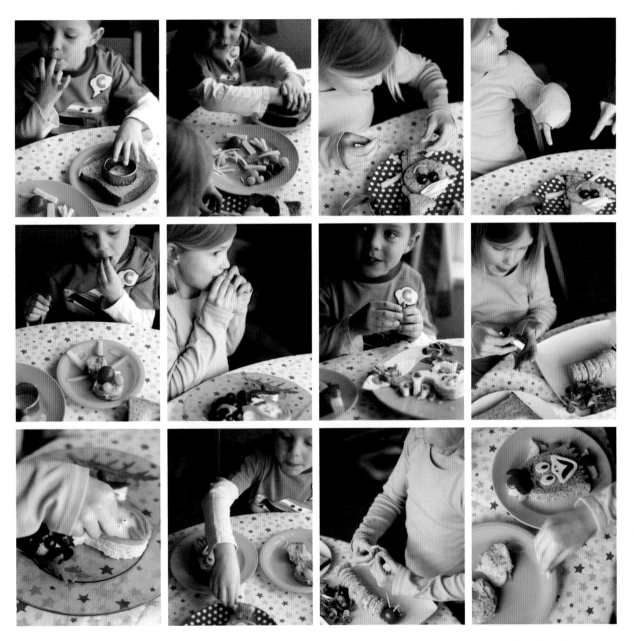

get funky

Templates The simplest way to get started with your funky lunch is by creating a template. Take a piece of paper or card and draw out the shape of a slice of bread so you know how big your design will be. Once you have the 'frame' for your lunch you can draw the shape you need and cut it out. Place your template on to your bread and use a knife or scissors to create your sandwich shape. A selection of templates to get you started can be found online at www.funkylunch.com/templates.

Tools I want Funky Lunch to be something that everybody can try at home, something that in essence requires a minimum amount of utensils and can be adapted to be as simple or as extravagant as you like. This is why the main tools in my sandwich-making kit consist of a small sharp knife, a vegetable peeler, an apple corer and a few shaped cutters. You don't need to go out and buy equipment, just improvise... if you can't find anything to cut small circles with, just clean up a few felt-tip pen lids and use those instead. Plasticine cutters can also come in a variety of shapes and sizes so are ideal for cutting out the smaller details you may need from things like cheese and vegetables. With a jam jar, a pen lid and a milk bottle top, you should be able to make the face, eyes and nose for a character. From there, the possibilities are endless....

Ingredients We all know how hard it can be sometimes to get children to eat the things that are good for them and I make no guarantee that your little ones will suddenly start munching down on fruit and vegetables after seeing this book; but even if it just sparks an interest in different foods, then surely that's a start? Don't stick to my recipes... get creative! If you know that no matter how hard you try they'll never eat a tomato, swap it for some red pepper. If they loathe carrot, substitute some Red Leicester. Similarly, if you want to introduce your child to new flavours, what better distraction for them? I've tried to suggest alternative ingredients as we go, but you know your child best so give them what you think will grab their attention and make them want to try it.

Finally... Some of the recipes here take more time and effort than others. They're designed for all occasions from quick, midday snacks to party time treats. You should adapt them in whichever way suits you and come up with your own inventions. And when you have, send them through to me and I'll post the best ones on the website for everyone else to get funky with.... Enjoy!

munch@funkylunch.com

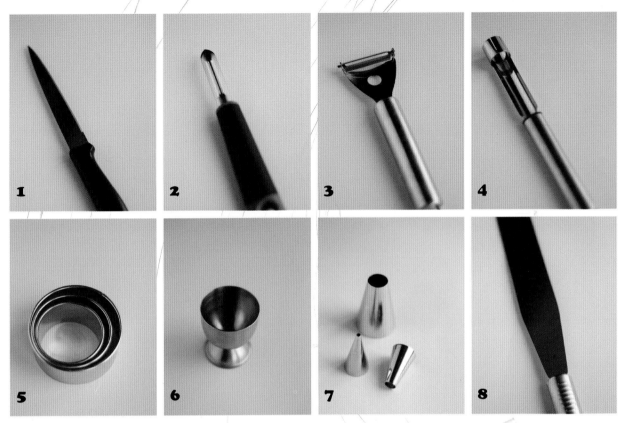

Tools of my trade
(1) a simple, sharp knife (2&3) vegetable peelers (4) apple corer (5,6&7) circle cutters...
in all shapes and sizes (8) a pallete knife – perfect for moving or flipping delicate things
(a fish slice is good too)

zoom, zoom, zoom!

Blasting off from a launch plate near you! A perfect little midday meal for the mini gastronaut in your life.

1 Assemble your sandwich using two slices of bread and your favourite filling.

2 Cut out the shape of the rocket with a sharp knife.

3 Carefully cut a square in the top layer of the bread and remove it for the window (the sandwich filling should show through). You can always fill this gap with a piece of ham, cheese or carrot.

4 Next, cut 2 'flame' shapes from a slice of carrot and top with a jagged piece of cheese to form the rocket booster.

5 Decorate your plate with some stars cut from cheese and a planet made from a slice of cucumber.

Try tomato or red pepper to give your rocket boosters a bit more crunch.

You will need • bread • sandwich filling • carrot • cucumber • cheese

chomp, chomp!

How many feet can you count as you munch your way through this little creation?

1 Make your sandwich using the bread and filling. The thicker you make the sandwich, the longer your caterpillar will appear in length.

2 Using a small circle cutter or egg cup, about 4cm across, cut as many circles from the sandwich as possible. Start in the corners to get the most from your bread and then arrange each circle of sandwich next to each other on their sides.

3 Cut 4 slices of cucumber about 5mm thick and then quarter each slice to give you 16 feet segments. Place 8 feet on each side of the body and trim down in size if they are too big.

4 Slice some cucumber lengthways and make 2 matchstick-size pieces for the antennae. Use a cocktail stick to make 2 holes on the top of the tomato and poke the antennae into the holes to hold them upright.

5 Using the remainder of the sliced cucumber and a small circle cutter, make 2 eyes and a half-moon-shaped mouth and stick these to the tomato face using the cream cheese. Finish off the eyes by sticking on small circles of grape skin.

As the sandwich pieces are standing on their side a filling such as cream cheese should help to hold them together and keep them in place.

Instead of cucumber feet and antennae, try carrot or celery for a sturdy substitute. You can also use cheese for the eyes and mouth.

You will need • bread • sandwich filling • cucumber • (good size) cherry tomato • red grape • cream cheese

yo ho ho!

Set sail on the high seas, *me hearty*, with this edible pirate adventure.

1 Assemble your sandwich using two slices of bread and your favourite filling.

2 Cut the shape of the ship's hull from your sandwich.

3 Take an apple corer and carefully make three portholes in the side of the ship's hull, removing just the top layer of bread.

4 Place the sandwich on a plate and use the breadsticks to form a mast and use the slice of ham for the sail.

5 Finish your sandwich with a skull-and-crossbones flag made from cucumber and cheese and then set it to sail on a sea of cucumber slices.

A sea of lettuce leaves makes a great alternative to cucumber.

Instead of a ham sail, use a slice of cheese for a meat-free alternative.

You will need • bread • sandwich filling • bread sticks • ham • cucumber • cheese

two scoops

Who says you can't give them ice cream for lunch? Just make sure they finish this one first!

1 Assemble your favourite sandwich using one slice of normal bread and a crust and cut this into the shape of an ice-cream cone.

2 Make another sandwich and with a small cup or cookie cutter, cut two circles from the sandwich.

3 Using the same sized cutter, cut a circle out of the cheese and a circle out of the ham too.

4 To assemble your ice-cream, place the ham slice on top of one of the sandwich circles and the cheese slice onto the other sandwich circle. Then position the two circles above the cone-shaped sandwich on your plate.

5 Finish it off by cutting a slice of cucumber to stick in the top.

For mint choc-chip ice cream, try using slices of green apple with the skin on, decorated with raisins.

You can use a slice of wholemeal bread for the cone if they won't eat the crust.

You will need •bread •crust of bread •sandwich filling •cheese •ham •cucumber

fresh as a daisy

Bring a little flower power to lunchtimes by serving up this blooming marvellous sandwich.

1 Make two sandwiches using your favourite fillings.

2 Using a cup or cookie cutter as big as you can fit on your sandwich and cut both into large circles.

3 With an apple corer, cut out a small circle from the centre of each sandwich but only remove the top layer of bread.

4 To make the petals for each flower, work around the sandwich making thin v-shaped cuts and removing the excess. Do this six or seven times until you have worked around each sandwich circle.

5 Take a cherry tomato and carefully remove the skin with a sharp knife in one piece. Now roll up this thin strip of tomato skin and place it into the centre of the sandwich, allowing it to loosely unroll a little.

6 For the stalks and leaves of your flowers, remove a strip of cucumber skin using a potato peeler and then carefully cut this into thin strips and place below your flowers.

7 Take some slices of cucumber and cut a few leaf shapes out and place at the bottom of the stalks along with a strip of cucumber skin cut into pointed blades of grass down one side.

Make cutting easier by using a clean pair of scissors, rather than a knife, to make the grass and leaf shapes.

Thin slices of spring onion or chives are a good alternative for the stems and grass.

You will need • bread • sandwich filling • cherry tomato • cucumber • cheese or carrot

make it snappy!

Get used to your little ones ordering *croc-monsieurs* from now on....

1 The crocodile is made by cutting two separate shapes from one sandwich and joining them together. Make your sandwich and cut it in half from top to bottom, then with the first half cut the body and head shape (it should resemble a stretched-out snowman). Cut out the long, curved tail section from the other sandwich half, ensuring the widest end of the tail section matches the width of the base of the body section.

2 Arrange both sandwich pieces on a plate and using a peeler to remove some skin from a cucumber, lay it down the length of the crocodile from head to tail until it is covered. Use a pair of clean scissors to trim the cucumber to match the body shape.

3 For the teeth, cut a wedge from the skinned cucumber and taper it at one end (this will form the back of the mouth).

4 Trim the other end to match the shape of the mouth and then use a small sharp knife to cut carefully across and through the cucumber at angles to form teeth. Remove the excess cucumber to leave you with an open mouth and sharp-looking teeth.

5 Open up the sandwich at the head end and insert the cucumber teeth between the two slices. You may need to trim some cucumber off the top and bottom of the mouth to make it fit without tearing the bread.

6 To make the eyes cut semi-circular wedges of cheese or cucumber and finish with cucumber skin pupils.

7 Finally, cut a slice of cucumber about 1cm thick and then quarter it. Use these quarters and carve some toes to make the feet.

Swap cucumber skin for thin slices of celery to give your croc some crunchy scales.

If cutting the teeth seems too tricky, use small triangles of cucumber or apple to fill up the mouth.

You will need • bread • sandwich filling • cucumber • cheese
(The crocodile shape is a bit tricky, but you can download a template from the Funky Lunch website. See page 8 for details.)

creepy crawly

They'll be taking more than just incy-wincy bites out of this lunchtime treat.

1 Slice open and make up the roll using your favourite filling.

2 Take a sharp knife and gently cut a shallow big smiling mouth shape into the top of the roll and remove just the crust.

3 Spread your cream cheese into the mouth area and smooth it out to leave some big white teeth. You can use thin strips of cucumber skin to define the lines between the teeth.

4 Cut two circles from a slice of cheese and top with two halves of black grape to make the eyes.

5 A spider would not be a spider without his legs, so using cucumber skin again, cut eight legs and tuck them into position underneath the roll.

Instead of cheese and grape eyes, try cucumber and olive instead.

If you don't want to use a roll, just cut a sandwich into a circle.

You will need • wholemeal roll • sandwich filling • cheese • cream cheese • black grapes • cucumber

home sweet home

Plate one of these up for lunch and encourage them to eat you out of house and home.

1 Make the sandwich using 2 slices of bread and your filling and then cut it into a basic house shape.

2 Cut the crust into a triangular roof shape and place it on top of the house. Make a chimney stack from the leftover crust and cut at an angle to match the slope of the roof.

3 Take a slice of cheese and cut it into three equal-sized small squares for the windows.

4 Slice three sides off a cherry tomato and then cut each slice in half. Trim the six pieces of tomato down until they match the size of your windows and then shape one side in a curve to finish the curtains.

5 Remove a large section of cucumber skin and trim it into a rectangle to make the front door.

6 With the leftover cucumber skin, cut 6 thin strips to mark out the window panes.

7 Finish with a few flowers cut from cheese, tomato and cucumber and a couple of roughly torn pieces of bread can be used for chimney smoke.

Use flower-shaped pastry or plasticine cutters to decorate the plate.

Use square slices of apple for the windows and pepper slices for the front door.

You will need • wholemeal bread (slices and crust) • sandwich filling • cheese • cherry tomato • cucumber

oink, oink!

Stave off the big bad wolf of hunger by serving up these cute little piggies for their lunch.

1 Before making your sandwich, take a large circular cookie cutter and cut a big circle from one slice of bread for the body. Using a smaller cutter, make another circle for the head. Use butter and sandwich filling to stick these two pieces together.

2 From the leftover bread cut two small ears and a smaller oval shape for the snout. Cut the same oval shape from a piece of ham to and lay it on top the oval of bread. Cut two pieces of ham to fit the shape of the ears.

3 To make the nostrils, push two holes right through the ham and bread of the snout using a small cutter or chopstick.

4 To layer up your sandwich, first place some cucumber skin beneath where the nostrils go and then place your bread and ham nose back over the top. You should then be able to see the dark cucumber skin through the nostril holes.

5 Finish your sandwich by making some eyes from discs of cheese and cucumber and finish with a twist of carrot for the tail.

Raisins make a great alternative for their miniature eyes.

To get a perfect curly tail, soak a strip of carrot in cold water for a few minutes and then wrap around a pencil and leave for a few minutes longer.

You will need • bread • sandwich filling • ham • cheese • cucumber • carrot

baaaaaaaaaa!

These scrummy sheep should help ensure your flock are eating and not bleating at the lunch table.

1 Make your sandwich using the wholemeal bread cutting a tapered rectangle with one end rounded for the nose and cut two small semi-circles for the ears.

2 Next, cut a cloud shape for the top of his woolly head from the slice of white bread.

3 Using a small circle cutter, gently make 2 holes in the nose. Then cut 2 same sized circles from a slice of cucumber skin and push these into the nose holes on the bread.

4 From a slice of cheese, make 2 oval eyes and then finish with 2 small circles of cucumber skin.

Replace cucumber nose and eyes with green pepper or grapes.

Instead of using bread for the hair and ears, why not try using a slice of cheese cut to shape.

You will need • **wholemeal bread** • **50/50 white bread** • **sandwich filling** • **cucumber** • **cheese**

an aquatic taste

These sweet little sea creatures should enchant even the most stubborn of appetites.

1 Make your sandwich and then, using a sharp knife, carefully cut out the head, body and tail shape of your mermaid in one piece.

2 Lay the cheese slice on the top half of her body and trim round the shape with a knife or clean scissors.

3 To make the hair, use the darker orange cheese and cut around the outside of her head to match the face slice and then, using a sharp knife, gently carve out the hairline around her face as in the picture. Place some strands of shredded carrot on top.

4 Peel some skin from a cucumber and use it to make the scales on her tail.

5 Finish your mermaid with some small slices of grape for her bikini top and small cucumber eyes and mouth.

Make the rocks by using half an apple topped with halved grapes.

If you can't find any orange cheese, just use more strands of carrot for the hair.

You will need • bread • sandwich filling • cheese slice • orange cheese (red leicester's perfect) • carrot • red grapes • cucumber

all aboard!

Sit back and watch them chew-chew their way through this little train.

1 Make your train sandwich using the brown bread and filling and then use a sharp knife to cut out a simple train shape.

2 Take one of the offcut lengths of crust and place it along the bottom of the train.

3 Carefully cut away and remove an area of the top slice of bread to create a window.

4 Cut 3 round slices of cucumber and trim them down if necessary to use for the wheels. Tuck them in between the sandwich slices so just over half a circle is showing.

5 Remove some long strips of cucumber skin using a potato peeler and then, using a sharp knife, cut the skin into long thin strips and use it to give the train some markings around the engine and funnel.

6 You can finish by laying down some cucumber tracks, a carrot for the dome on top and some fluffy clouds of steam from the slice of white bread.

Turn this sandwich into a long party platter by making lots of carriage sandwiches and attaching them onto one another in a long line.

You will need • bread • sandwich filling • cucumber • cheese • carrot

twit twoo

They'll have a hoot eating this wide-eyed, feathery feast.

1 Make your favourite sandwich using the filling of your choice and then cut it into an oval shape – a bit like an egg.

2 From the top layer of the sandwich, cut a small oval shape, starting from the bottom of the owl's body, to just over halfway up. Gently remove this top layer of bread and then, using your slice of white bread, cut a shape to match the piece you have just removed.

3 Place the white bread oval into the gap on the sandwich and then, using a small knife or cocktail stick, scratch around the join of the white bread and brown to merge the two pieces together so it looks like a feathered edge.

4 To make the eyes, cut the outline of a number 8 and turn it on its side. Finish the eyes with two small circles of cucumber skin.

5 From a thin slice of carrot, cut a triangle shape and rest this in place for the beak.

6 The feet can be cut from a small wedge of carrot and then cut small V-shapes to form the claws.

7 Decorate your plate with a breadstick tree branch and then sit your owl onto the plate in position.

Try using two slices of hard-boiled egg for the eyes as the white and yellow make a perfect base for your wide-eyed owl.

You will need • wholemeal bread • 50/50 white bread • sandwich filling • cheese • carrot • cucumber • breadstick

flutter by

A nicer species of butterflies for the tummy! These ones should allow their hunger to take flight pronto.

1 Cut out the shape of a butterfly from your prepared sandwich.

2 To make the body, use a slice of cheese and cut it into a pencil shape with a point at one end and a round head at the other.

3 Using thin strips of cucumber skin you can give your butterfly a stripy body, smiling face and antennae.

4 Now get your assortment of tomato, carrot, pepper and cucumber pieces and decorate your butterfly to your own design.

Instead of vegetable decorations, use red and green apple slices, grapes, blueberries and more for a special fruity twist.

Give your child the basic sandwich shape and a selection of colourful vegetables and let them create their own patterns, eating as they go.

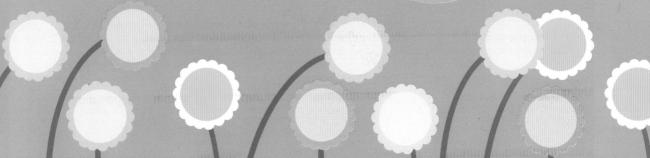

You will need • bread • sandwich filling • cheese • tomato • pepper • carrot • cucumber

nessy

Perfect for putting to rest the rumbling bellies of little monsters.

1 Slice your bagel in half and prepare it using your favourite filling (cream cheese helps to hold it all together well).

2 Cut your bagel in half to give you two semi-circles and place one on its side to form the back of the monster.

3 Taking the other half of the bagel, cut it into two and round off one end for the head. Cut the other piece into a pointed tail, still using the curve of the bagel for the shape.

4 Make a small hole in the side of the sea monster's head and fill it with cream cheese and a small cucumber skin circle for the eye. Perforate the front of the head with two holes and put a tiny round of cucumber skin into each for the nostrils. Use a knife to cut a slit into the bottom of the head and then fill with a slice of cucumber (skin side outwards) to form a mouth.

5 Remove some slices of skin from a cucumber and cut about twelve triangle shapes from them. Tuck these shapes in between the bagel slices to form the spikes along his back.

Stabilise the head by 'cementing' the pieces to the plate with cream cheese or propping it up with a cocktail stick (remove the stick before you serve).

You will need • bagels (as perfectly round as possible) • bagel filling • cucumber • cream cheese

tall order

Make sure their lunch is head and shoulders above the rest, with this cute giraffe.

1 Make your sandwich using two slices of bread and your favourite filling, and then cut out the giraffe head shape.

2 Take a third slice of bread, cut an oval shape to form the giraffe's nose area and with the leftover bread, cut a long rectangle to use as the neck.

3 Before putting the nose in place, make two holes using an apple corer for nostrils and place some thin strips of cucumber skin underneath the holes on top of the main sandwich.

4 Take your crust and cut the shape of the forehead at one end and with the remainder, cut out two horns and some circles of different sizes and place on the neck.

5 Give your giraffe some eyes and a mouth made from cucumber skin.

Use a slice of brown bread for the giraffe features, instead of the crust.

Black grapes or olives make a simple alternative for the eyes and nose.

You will need • bread • crust of bread • sandwich filling • cucumber

king of the jungle

Rooaarring on to their plates, this beast of a feast will keep your wild ones full until teatime.

1 Assemble your sandwich using the slices of bread and filling.

2 Cut out the head shape from the sandwich and then use a piece of the leftover bread to form a triangle shape for a nose.

3 For the eyes, use oval-shaped pieces of sliced cucumber and finish each eye with half a black grape.

4 Take a slice of cucumber skin and mirror the shape of the bread nose as you cut, then lay over the top. Use a thin slice of cucumber skin to make the mouth.

5 For the lion's mane, take some slices of cheese and some carrot sliced lengthways and make lots of triangle shapes. Tuck these shapes in between the layers of sandwich, alternating between cheese and carrot to get a good mix of colour.

Avoid your bread drying out by cutting all of your triangles of carrot and cheese before you begin making your sandwich.

You will need • bread • sandwich filling • cheese • carrot • cucumber • black grapes

happy birthday!

Ensure many happy returns to the lunch table by serving up these impressive little cakes.

1 Make two sandwiches using the bread and your favourite fillings.

2 Cut each sandwich into a circle using a large cookie cutter or cup.

3 Cut the carrot into four sticks about 5cm long by 5mm wide and then cut a small section out of one end to make the candles.

4 Take a slice of cheese and cut four small flames and slot them into the top of the candles.

5 Place the two sandwiches on top of each other and then decorate around the base using halves of cherry tomato or grapes. Cut the birthday numbers you need from a slice of cucumber skin.

Make a large platter of little cakes and serve them as party nibbles.

Use a mix of white and red grapes or cherry tomatoes for decoration.

You will need • bread • sandwich filling • cheese • carrot • cucumber • cherry tomatoes or grapes

go bananas!

A wholesome treat for the little monkeys in your life.

1 Make your sandwich using your favourite filling and the bread.

2 Turn the sandwich so the crust is facing up and then cut out the shape of the monkey's head.

3 To make the face and ear sections, cut carefully into the crust and remove the top layer of the crust only, without cutting all the way through the slice.

4 Once the top layer of crust has been removed, make two eyes from small ovals of cheese and cucumber skin.

5 Finish your monkey by using more cucumber skin for the nostrils and smiling mouth.

Decorate the plate with pieces of banana to give it a fruity flavour.

It might be easier to make the sandwich with 2 slices of wholemeal bread and then cut an oval from a crust and place it on top of the nose area.

You will need • bread (including crust) • sandwich filling • cheese • cucumber

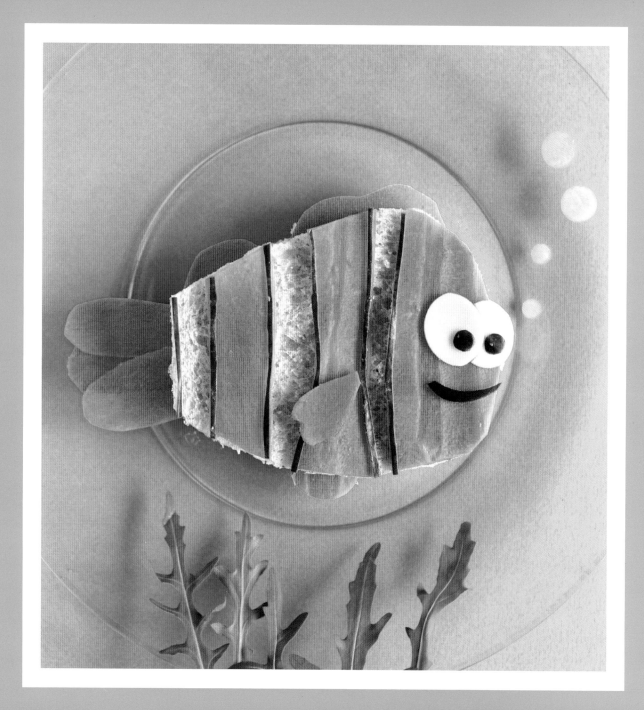

catch of the day

A fishy treat to reel in and eat!

1 Make your fishy sandwich using the bread and filling.

2 Cut it into an oval shape, slightly tapered at one end.

3 Take a carrot and, using a peeler, make long strips of carrot that will cover the body.

4 Starting at the head, place two strips of carrot next to each other in a vertical direction and leave a small gap and then another two strips of carrot and then leave a bigger gap before finishing with one more strip and a small gap at the tail end.

5 Using a pair of clean scissors, trim off any excess carrot that over-hangs the edge of the fish body.

6 Use three smaller strips of carrot with round edges and tuck them between the sandwich layers to form a tail. Using the same idea, make three rounded fins and tuck into place.

7 Cut the white part from a couple of cucumber slices to make two over-lapping eyes. Cut the pupils from cucumber skin and cut a small strip of cucumber for the mouth.

8 Finish your fish by accentuating the white stripes of the body with thin borders of cucumber skin.

9 Decorate your plate with bubbles made from thin circles of cucumber and some rocket or lettuce leaves for seaweed.

Decorate the plate with a few bubbles made from thin circles of cucumber.

You will need • bread • sandwich filling • carrot • cucumber • rocket or lettuce leaves

santa's little helper

This festive feast uses toasted antlers to give Rudolph a touch of added crunch.

1 Make your sandwich using your favourite filling and two slices of bread, and then cut out the head shape.

2 From a third slice of bread, cut out a letter 'B' shape and place on its side at the bottom end of the head, place a small slice of cucumber skin in between for the mouth. Cut two petal shapes from the leftover bread to make his ears and then two smaller-sized petals from the crust part of the bread for the inner ear detail.

3 To make the antlers, toast another slice of bread and then cut out two jagged shapes and position at the top of the head.

4 Create two eyes from circles of cheese and place half a black grape on each one.

5 Finish off your reindeer with a trademark red nose, made from a cherry tomato.

Be daring! Try black olives for the eyes instead of grapes.

Instead of a big juicy tomato nose, try a radish or a circular cut of red pepper.

You will need • brown bread • filling • cherry tomato • cheese

great white bite

Let your little sea urchins dive in and sink their jaws into these great white shark sandwiches!

1 Make your sandwich and then cut the head of your shark out of the bread so it looks like a triangle with round edges.

2 Take the leftover cuts of bread and make 3 fins and a tail from a single layer of the bread and put them in place on your plate.

3 To make the shark's mouth, cut the top layer and remove the bread to form an opening.

4 From two strips of cucumber or cheese, cut and remove small triangles leaving you with a row of sharp teeth.

5 Lift the top layer of bread and place a strip of cucumber skin on top of the sandwich filling where the mouth opening will be and then place the two rows of teeth on top. Replace the bread layer making sure the teeth and dark background can be seen through the opening.

6 Finish your shark with two menacing eyes made from cheese and cucumber and two tiny cucumber nostrils will complete this underwater treat.

Add a few jellyfish, made from thinly sliced halves of cucumber and strips of carrot.

You will need • bread • sandwich filling • cucumber • cheese

pretty polly

Let them get their beaks into these colourful characters and help keep them quiet for a while!

1 Make your sandwich using your favourite ingredients and cut out the shape of your parrot. You could use a hand drawn template to help you.

2 Cut some thin slices of cucumber lengthways and lay these on top of your sandwich. Trim the cucumber so it matches the outline of your bread.

3 To make the feathery wings, use wide thin slices of cheese, carrot and cucumber skin and give each piece a zig-zag end making sure that you stagger each slice as you layer them up.

4 Using a slice of carrot from the widest part, trim it to match the shape of the head.

5 Cut a small piece of cheese for the beak and then add some cucumber eyes.

6 The parrot's claws are cut from a thick chunk of carrot, leaving enough room to fit a breadstick perch in place.

Serve your parrot sandwich with a bowl of nuts, seeds or rasins to nibble on.

You will need • bread • sandwich filling • cheese • carrot • cucumber

feline peckish?

These little kitten sandwiches really are the cat's whiskers.

1 Make your sandwich using your favourite filling and then cut out an oval shape with two pointed ears for the head.

2 Peel off some lengths of cucumber skin and cut 6 thin strips and poke into the bread to hold the whiskers in place.

3 Cut 2 small eyes from cucumber skin and make the nose from circles of cucumber and cheese. Make the mouth from a piece of cucumber skin cut into a curved '3' shape.

4 Finally, cut 2 triangles of ham and place one inside each of the ear shapes.

Thin slices of spring onion are also perfect for a smart set of whiskers.

For a treat without meat, replace the little pink ham ears with red apple.

You will need •bread •sandwich filling •cucumber •cheese •ham

hop to it!

Indulge in a little midday magic by pulling this rabbit out of your lunchtime hat.

1 Make your rabbit sandwich using two slices of bread and the filling and cut out an oval shape for the head.

2 Take a third slice of bread and cut out the ear shapes and place them into position on the plate.

3 Make two eyes by cutting oval shapes from a slice of cheese. Add pupils by cutting smaller oval shapes from cucumber skin.

4 Cut a small circular slice of tomato for the nose and use a piece of cucumber skin for the mouth.

5 Make the rabbit's teeth by cutting a small slice of cheese into two rectangles.

Decorate the plate with mini carrots by cutting wedges of carrot and using cucumber skin for the carrot tops.

You will need • bread • sandwich filling • cucumber • cheese • tomato • carrot

tentacled treat

Arm yourself more than adequately for lunch with this under-the-sea spectacular sandwich.

1 Use your favourite filling and two slices of bread to make your sandwich. Then from it cut the octopus head and the two front tentacles in one piece.

2 Take another slice of bread and cut 6 more tentacle shapes and place them behind the front two on each side.

3 Slice the skin off some tomatoes and use a smaller circular cutter to make approximately twelve small circles or semi-circles. Place these little 'suckers' onto the tentacles, trimming the tomato to make them fit.

4 Make the eyes, eyebrows and mouth from the skin and flesh of some cucumber.

5 Decorate your plate with a sea bed made from cheese and lettuce leaf seaweed.

When layering the tentacles, squash a couple of them down flat so they appear to be behind the ones in front.

You will need • bread • sandwich filling • tomato • cucumber • cheese • lettuce

dairy delights

Your little herd will be over the moo-oon grazing over these.

1 Before making the sandwich, place 2 wholemeal slices of bread together and cut out the shape of the head excluding the ears.

2 With the top slice of wholemeal, cut away the centre section leaving 2 side areas for the eyes.

3 Cut a slice of white bread to fit on the head with a narrow section in the middle to allow the sides to fit on.

4 Using the leftover white bread, cut the outline of a number '8' for the nose and then cut two ears from the leftover brown bread.

5 To assemble, butter your bottom layer of bread and place the sandwich filling on top, then butter and place the main white section and the two brown sides into position.

6 Turn the nose section on its side and make two holes in each side and fill with small pieces of cucumber skin to look like nostrils and put into place.

7 Make two eyes using cucumber flesh, with skin for the pupils and finally tuck a small piece of ham underneath the nose-shaped piece of bread for the tongue.

Cheese and grapes make a tasty alternative for the eyes.

Instead of ham for the tongue you could use a pink piece of apple skin.

You will need • white and brown bread • sandwich filling • cucumber • ham

clowning around

Put on a big lunchtime performance with these bright and cheery little clowns.

1 Make your sandwich and cut it into a round or oval face shape.

2 Make the eyes using a disc of cheese cut into oval shapes and then use a small circular cutter to make two discs of cucumber skin for the pupils.

3 Take a large round cutter and from a wide slice of cheese cut out a circle. Take a slightly smaller cutter and cut another circle out of the middle of the first. Cut the remaining ring of cheese in half and round the edges off to make a big smiling mouth.

4 Grate a large carrot and bunch up the strands on each side of the clown's head. Cut two slices of carrot and score each with a knife to shape into bushy eyebrows.

5 Place the cherry tomato into the centre of your clown's face and then compose the other parts around it.

6 Finish the sandwich by laying two triangular chunks of cucumber alongside one circular chunk of cucumber to form a bow tie.

Before eating, have fun trying different hair styles using the grated carrot.

Try using yellow pepper or big slices of red or green apple to make his bow tie.

You will need • bread • **sandwich filling** • **carrot** • **cheese** • **cucumber** • cherry tomato

crust-aceous lunch

Perfect for the little nippers in the family.

1 Before making your pitta bread sandwich, cut the shape of the crabs body being careful to save both leftover side pieces.

2 Gently open your pitta and fill with your favourite ingredients.

3 Using the leftover pitta bread, cut out two oval shapes and then cut a zig-zag down the middle of each one; pull open at this cut to show off his big claws.

4 Slice 6 thick lengths of cucumber skin and cut each one into a curved point.

5 Arrange the 6 cucumber legs and two pitta claws on a plate and then place the crab's body over the top.

6 From a slice of cheese, make two eyes and a mouth, then finish with cucumber eyebrows and black grape pupils.

Pitta bread suits the crab's shape well, but you could use either a roll or sliced bread instead.

For a fruitier creature, swap the cheese eyes and mouth for slices of apple.

You will need • pitta bread • sandwich filling • cheese • cucumber • black grapes

out of this world

They'll need taste buds from another planet to refuse this extraterrestrial treat.

1 Make your sandwich using your favourite filling and then cut a large circle as big as you can get from your bread.

2 Gently, cut a smiling mouth out of the top layer of the sandwich. Then take two slices of cheese, cutting squares into the edge of each slice for a row of teeth. Cut a length of cucumber skin to the same size as the mouth. Carefully slide the skin and then, on top, the two rows of teeth inbetween the bread layers so as to show through the cavity made for the mouth.

3 To make the eyes, cut three small thin strips of cucumber skin and arrange in place, then using a small cutter or clean pen lid, cut three small circles of cucumber flesh and three circles of cucumber skin.

4 Slice off a piece of cherry tomato and decorate with three nostril holes.

5 Make the arms and legs by slicing some strips of carrot lengthways and then cutting into shape.

6 Decorate your plate with a cheese moon and some cheese stars too if you have a cutter to hand.

You don't have to stop at three eyes, let your alien imagination run wild.

Use a black grape for the nose if tomatoes are not a favourite.

You will need • bread • sandwich filling • cheese • cucumber • cherry tomato • carrot

cock-a-doodle-do

Another farmyard favourite guaranteed to have them clucking for more.

1 Assemble your sandwich using the bread and fillings and then cut a shape that is rounded at the top and has a zigzag pattern at the other end.

2 Using a small circular cutter, make two circles from a slice of cheese to form the eyes. Finish these off with two smaller circles of cucumber skin.

3 Take another slice of cheese and carefully cut the beak out to match the picture, removing a centre piece for the open mouth.

4 Before laying the cheese beak on to the sandwich, remove some cucumber skin and lay this into place first and then rest the beak on top. Make sure that the cucumber skin can be seen through the hole in the mouth.

5 Take a sharp knife and slice a thick layer of skin from a tomato. Press flat on a chopping board and then cut the tomato into a teardrop shape. Repeat this three more times and arrange three red 'feathers' on top of the head.

6 Place the last tomato feather on its chin and use some thin strips of cucumber skin for eyebrows and nostrils to finish.

You may find it easier to cut the tomato shapes with a small clean pair of scissors, instead of a sharp knife.

If your tomato is too squashy, use some red pepper instead for the feathers, as this will add crunch and be easier to cut.

You will need • bread • sandwich filling • cheese slices • cherry tomatoes • cucumber

sounds delicious

Give your little maestros a standing ovation, for finishing this tuneful treat.

1 The outline of the piano has two straight edges – one on the left and one across the bottom and a curved step shape that starts in the top left and goes down to the bottom right. Before making your sandwich, place both slices of bread together and cut out the piano shape.

2 Using the top slice of bread, cut along the bottom edge a strip about 1cm wide and remove. This is where the keys will sit. Cut a similar sized section from the same edge so that you are left with the curved lid and a strip of bread.

3 Butter and lay your filling on the other slice of bread, leaving room at the bottom straight edge to place a strip of cheese for the keyboard. Butter and stick the thin strip of bread behind the keys.

4 Cut three rectangular chunks of carrot into sturdy legs and place flat on a plate. Now rest the bottom layer of sandwich carefully on top of the legs so that it is sitting in position.

5 Using a thin stick of carrot, gently balance the small curved lid at an angle on top of the bottom slice.

6 To make the keys, press the tip of a cocktail stick into the strip of cheese to form small grooves and then with very thin slices of cucumber skin, cut small rectangles for the black keys.

Try using sticks of cucumber or celery to prop up your piano top.

The cheese and cucumber keyboard can be made in advance before placing it on the piano.

You will need • bread • filling • cheese • cucumber • carrot
(The shape of the body of the piano is a bit tricky, but you can download a template from the Funky Lunch website. See page 8 for details.)

up in the clouds

A colourful treat for when you're stuck inside on a blustery day.

1 Before making your sandwich, place a slice of white bread and a slice of brown together and cut out a diamond shape for your kite. Cut each slice across the width and length of the shape and then swap the top and bottom slices of bread around in one half of the top section and do the same in the opposite half of the bottom section, so you end up with a pattern that looks like ours.

2 Use butter and filling to make the four sections of sandwich and then place each section into position on your plate.

3 Cut some small thin rectangular slices of carrot and then trim each piece into a bow shape. Do the same with a slice of cheese so you end up with approximately 7 carrot bows and 5 cheese bows.

4 Remove a long thin slice of cucumber skin and cut it into a long strip to make the tail and then place five of each bow along its length.

5 Cut two more ribbon pieces of cucumber skin and attach these to the middle of the kite along with two thin strips of carrot topped with the final two carrot bows.

6 Finally, attach two more lengths of carrot ribbon to the base of the kite and then decorate your plate with a little cloud in the sky made from roughly torn white bread.

Chives or thin spring onions make good substitute ribbons.

Let them decorate the kite's tail using their favourite fruit or vegetables.

You will need • brown and white bread • filling • cheese • cucumber • carrot

take things slowly

A lunchtime treat for your little gastro-pods. This great sandwich idea was created by Funky follower, Theresa Croyle from Forest Lake, Minnesota, USA.

1 Slice open your bagel and pack it with a sandwich filling that will hold it together once upright.

2 Trim the wide end of a celery stick at an angle to form the head and cut the tail end of it to your desired length.

3 Cut a 'V' shape into one of the edges on the bagel so it sits nicely along your celery stick.

4 Using the offcuts of celery, make two thin sticks and fix them into the 'head' end of the celery by cutting a small slit each side and pushing them in place.

5 To make the eyes, cut a black grape in half and, using a small circular cutter, remove the middle of the grape and replace with a small circle of cheese, topped with a spot of grape skin for the pupil.

6 Using a small pointed knife, make a hole in the bottom of the grape eye and push this on top of the celery stick.

7 Decorate your snail's shell with thin strips of spring onion held in place with either butter or cream cheese.

For a genuine (albeit grisly!) touch, spread a trail of snail 'slime' behind your snail using a squirt of relish.

Dress your plate with lettuce leaves to get a real garden feel.

You will need •bagel •filling •celery •grapes •spring onion •cheese

down periscope

Dive, dive, dive into lunchtime with this underwater adventure on a plate.

1 Slice your roll lengthways and fill with your favourite ingredients.

2 Using a small circular cutter, make three porthole shapes down one side of the roll and remove the bread and any filling.

3 With the same sized cutter, make 3 circular windows from a slice of cheese and a thin strip of cucumber skin around the edge.

4 To make the submarine's periscope, cut a chunky 'L' shape from a piece of carrot and then round off the edges. Scoop out the end and push a small circle of cucumber skin into place.

If you can't find a sub roll then a hot dog roll will make a good alternative.

Fill the portholes with something already to size such as grapes or a slice of radish.

You will need • sub roll • filling • carrot • cheese • cucumber

funky thanks

It's not often you get to thank your children for being stubborn, but without the grumbling of a 4-year-old boy on a sunny day in May, this whole chapter in my life would have drifted past unnoticed.

To Izzy and Oscar, thank you for eating what I put in front of you, and tasting things at least once, you are my inspiration and the reason why Funky Lunch works. To my wife Lisa, who never complains when she finds only half a carrot and a few skinned cucumbers left in the fridge and for allowing me to spend an entire family holiday chatting on my phone and laptop to the world's press.

To my unofficial PR mentor, Kelly Davies, whose off-the-cuff remark at the outset planted that first seed and for her enthusiastic tweeting which led me to Beth Murray, a complete stranger at the time, who on the promise of a sandwich placed me firmly in the media spotlight and started Funky Lunch on this rollercoaster ride. I still owe her that sandwich! Thank you ladies.

Huge appreciation goes to the team at Absolute Press for spotting the potential of Funky Lunch and believing in its concept. To Matt Inwood, whose tireless photography and design has captured the essence of this book perfectly and to the Inwood family for allowing me to commandeer their kitchen in the pursuit of sandwich excellence, thank you.

Finally, a special thanks to my friends and family whose encouragement and questioning of my sanity made me even more determined to succeed. To the hundreds and thousands of followers online, the blog writers, the tweeters, the Facebook devotees and everyone who has helped turn a simple idea into an amazing journey… I hope you enjoy this book.